A Gift from

THE FRED MEYER FOUNDATION

MEXICO ABCs

A Book About the People and Places of Mexico

Country ABCs

Written by Sarah Heiman
Illustrated by Todd Ouren

Mexico Advisor: Dr. Susan Schroeder
France V. Scholes Professor of Colonial Latin American History
Stone Center for Latin American Studies, Tulane University
New Orleans, Louisiana

Reading Advisor: Lauren A. Liang, M.A.
Literacy Education, University of Minnesota
Minneapolis, Minnesota

PiCTURE WiNDOW BOOKS
Minneapolis, Minnesota

Editor: Peggy Henrikson
Designer: Nathan Gassman
Page production: Picture Window Books
The illustrations in this book were prepared digitally.

Picture Window Books
5115 Excelsior Boulevard
Suite 232
Minneapolis, MN 55416
1-877-845-8392
www.picturewindowbooks.com

Printed in the United States of America.

Library of Congress Cataloging-in-Publication Data
Heiman, Sarah, 1955–
Mexico ABCs: a book about the people and places of Mexico / written by Sarah Heiman ; illustrated by Todd Ouren.
p. cm. — (Country ABCs)
ISBN 1-4048-0023-9 (library binding : alk. paper)
1. Mexico—Description and travel—Juvenile literature. 2. Mexico—Social life and customs—Juvenile literature.
I. Ouren, Todd. II. Title. III. Series.
F1216.5 .H54 2003
972—dc21
2002006278

Spanish words are in *italics*, except where they have been accepted into the English language or are proper nouns.

¡Hola! ¿Qué pasa? (OH-lah! Kay PAH-sah?)

That means "Hello! What's happening?" in Spanish, the main language of Mexico. Mexico is in North America, just south of the United States. More than 101 million people live in Mexico. It ranks 11th in world population.

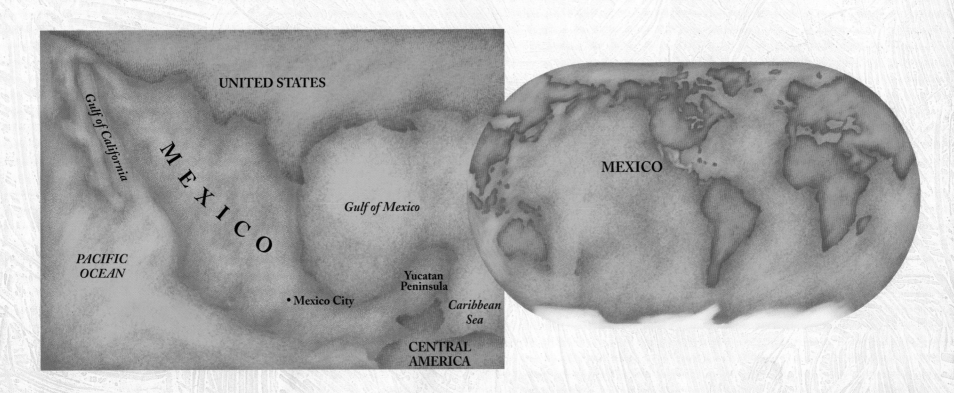

A is for art.

The colors and patterns of Mexican art are bright and bold.
Mural artists turn walls into huge paintings.

Some Mexican art looks like Spanish art, because Spain ruled Mexico from the early 1500s to 1821.

Other Mexican art looks like the art of the peoples living in Mexico before the Spaniards came.

These native peoples included the Aztecs, Zapotecs, and Mayas. Sometimes Mexican artists mix art styles.

B is for butterfly.

In autumn, monarch butterflies fly thousands of miles from Canada and the United States to the mountains of central Mexico. The butterflies cover pine and fir trees, and branches sometimes even break from their weight.

C is for Cinco de Mayo
(SEENG-ko day MYE-yoh).

Cinco de Mayo means the fifth of May. It's also the name of a festival held on that day. People dance in colorful costumes to celebrate a great day of victory in 1862. In that year, Mexican soldiers fought French invaders and won, even though the French had twice as many soldiers.

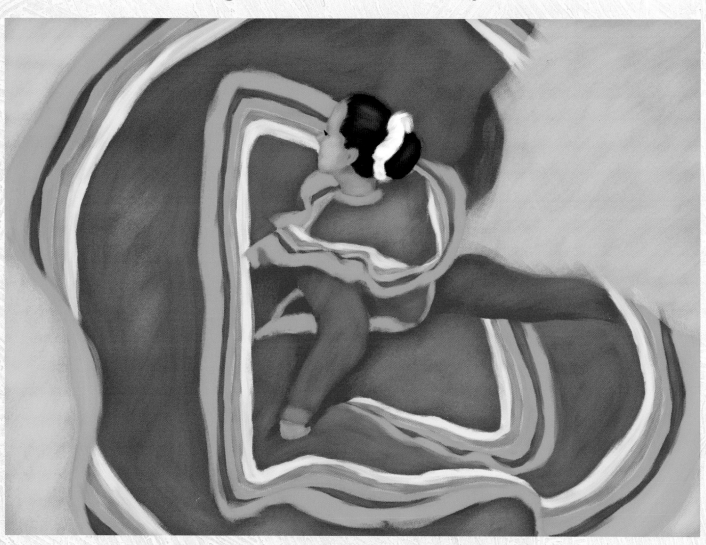

Another important national holiday is Independence Day, September 16. It marks the day in 1821 when Mexico won its freedom from Spain.

D is for Day of the Dead.

Day of the Dead is observed on November 2. Families picnic, plant flowers, and leave gifts at the graves of loved ones.

Cookies in the shape of skulls are a traditional Day of the Dead treat.

7

E is for enchilada (en-chuh-LAH-duh).

Enchiladas are a favorite food in Mexico. Meat, cheese, or beans are rolled up in a tortilla and then covered with a tomato sauce. See page 23 for more about tortillas.

F is for flag.

The green in Mexico's flag stands for hope. The white is for religion and purity. The red stands for unity and the blood of Mexicans who died fighting for freedom. In the middle of the flag is the country's coat of arms.

Legend of the Mexican Coat of Arms

The ancient Aztecs had a hummingbird god. This god told the people that a sign would let them know where to build a new city. They saw an eagle sitting on a cactus and eating a snake, and they knew this was the sign. The Aztecs began to build the capital of their nation on that spot in 1325. It is now Mexico City, the capital of Mexico.

G is for guitar.

The guitar, or *guitarra* (gee-TAH-rra), is a big part of traditional Mexican music. Guitarists lead popular dance bands called mariachi bands. The large bass guitar with the round back is called a *guittarón* (gee-tah-ROHN).

10

H is for hacienda (hah-see-EN-dah).

A hacienda is a large house in the country. Haciendas often have a patio or garden space in the center of the house.

In the country and small towns, houses traditionally were built with adobe, which is a kind of brick made of mud and straw.

I is for *iglesia* (ee-GLAY-see-ah).

A church, or *iglesia*, stands at the center of every Mexican community. Religion is so important to the Mexican people that a church was often the first building to be built in a town. Most of the people in Mexico are Roman Catholic.

The Spaniards brought the Roman Catholic religion when they came to Mexico in the early 1500s. Before that, the native peoples had their own religions. Some Mexicans still practice the native religions.

12

J is for Juárez (hwah-REZ).

Benito Juárez is a hero to many Mexicans. He was a Zapotec native and the first native person to be elected president of Mexico. He was president from 1861 until he died in 1872.

Benito Juárez

K is for kit fox.

Desert covers much of northern Mexico, where the kit fox lives. Besides the kit fox, you'll see prairie dogs, lizards, snakes, and scorpions in that part of Mexico.

Wildlife in Other Areas of Mexico

Rain forests: monkeys, parrots, jaguars, tapirs

Mountains: coyotes, wolves, deer, mountain lions

Oceans around Mexico: gray whales, tuna, swordfish, tropical fish, shrimp, manatees, pelicans

14

L is for lantern.

During the Christmas season in Mexico, the night is lit up with lanterns, or luminarias (loo-mih-NAIR-ee-ahs). People first made these special lights by setting a candle in sand inside a paper bag. Many luminarias are still made this way, but now they are also made of pottery and metal.

M is for money.

Mexico's unit of money is the *peso*, which comes in both coins and bills. One *peso* equals 100 *centavos*.

Nn

N is for nopal (noh-PAHL) cactus.

The nopal cactus is one of over 1,000 different kinds of cactus in Mexico. It has thick, flat leaves, and it grows in the Sonoran Desert of northwestern Mexico.

Mexicans cut nopal leaves into tiny pieces and fry them. Fried nopal and scrambled eggs make a good breakfast.

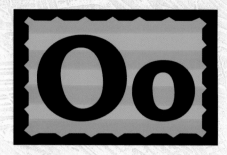

O is for outdoor market.

An outdoor market, or *mercado* (mair-CAH-doh), can be found in almost every Mexican town. You'll find everything from brightly painted wooden toys to pots, clothing, fruits, and vegetables.

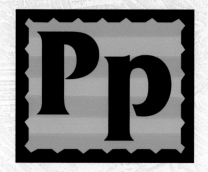

P **p**

P is for piñata (pee-NYAH-tah).

At birthdays and other celebrations in Mexico, a piñata hangs from the ceiling. It is filled with candies and small toys. One at a time, children are blindfolded and twirled around. Then each child swings hard at the piñata with a stick. When the piñata breaks, the treats spill out.

19

Q is for quetzal
(KATE-sahl).

The rain forests of southern Mexico are home to many birds and animals, including the quetzal. This bird was important to the Aztecs. They used quetzal feathers as money for trading. They also decorated their clothing with the brightly colored plumes.

R is for Río Grande.

This wide, shallow, slow-moving river forms nearly two-thirds of the border between Mexico and the United States. Early Spanish explorers first named this river the Río Grande, which means "big river." Americans still call it that, but Mexicans now call it the Río Bravo, or "bold river."

The Río Grande begins in the San Juan Mountains of Colorado. The river is 1,885 miles (3,034 kilometers) long and empties into the Gulf of Mexico at Brownsville, Texas.

S is for serape (say-RAH-pay).

Serapes are made of heavy wool and are worn over the shoulders. They can also be used as blankets on cool nights.

Other Traditional Mexican Clothing

sombrero: a wide-brimmed hat

chaleco: a woven vest

china poblana: a decorated skirt, blouse, and sash for traditional dances

T is for tortilla (tor-TEE-yah).

A tortilla is a flat, thin, round bread made from either wheat flour or cornmeal. Mexicans use it to scoop up food, or they wrap it around ground beef, cheese, and refried beans.

Other Mexican Favorites

chili: a soup or sauce made of hot chili peppers

tamales: cornmeal dough filled with spiced meat and steamed in a corn husk

mole: a thick, dark, spicy sauce, often flavored with chocolate and ground nuts

23

U is for *uno* (OO-noh).

Uno means one in Spanish. Try counting to ten in Spanish.

uno (OO-noh)

dos (DOHSS)

tres (TRAYSS)

cuatro (KWAH-troh)

cinco (SING-koh)

seis (SAYSS)

siete (see-AY-tay)

ocho (OH-cho)

nueve (noo-WAY-vay)

diez (dee-AYSS)

V is for Virgin of Guadalupe
(gwah-dah-LOO-pay).

Many homes in Mexico
have a picture or statue of
the Virgin of Guadalupe.
She is also known as Mary,
the mother of Jesus.
Catholics in Mexico believe
the Virgin of Guadalupe
keeps a loving eye on them.

The Lady of Guadalupe

Juan Diego was an Aztec farmer.
One morning in 1531, Juan heard a
woman call his name. She said she
was "the mother of all who live in
this land" and she wanted a church
built on the nearby hill. She showed
Juan a bush of beautiful roses. He'd
never seen roses growing there
before. He picked some and put
them inside his cloak, or *tilma*, to
show the bishop. When he opened
his *tilma*, he found a beautiful
painting of the lady on the cloak.
Today Juan's cloak, with its picture
of the Virgin of Guadalupe, hangs
in a church that was built next to
that hill.

W w

W is for warrior.

In 1502 a warrior, or soldier, named Montezuma II became the leader of the Aztec people. While he was emperor, the Aztecs controlled more than half of the area that is now Mexico.

Aztec emperor and warrior Montezuma II

X x

X is for Xochimilco (SOH-chee-MEEL-koh).

Visitors come from all over to enjoy the beauty of Lake Xochimilco. They ride in brightly painted boats that glide through a maze of colorful island gardens.

Long ago, the Aztecs covered reed rafts with mud and planted them with fruits, vegetables, and flowers. Over the years, the plants' roots grew down into the lake. The rafts formed islands, which are still gardens today.

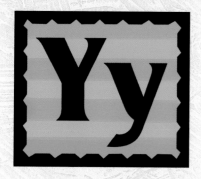

Y is for Yucatan Peninsula.

The Yucatan Peninsula reaches like a big thumb into the Gulf of Mexico and the Caribbean Sea. Its white, sandy beaches and ancient Mayan ruins draw tourists by the thousands. Tulum and Chichen Itza are two famous ruins.

A step pyramid at the Chichen Itza ruins on the Yucatan Peninsula

27

Z is for *zócalo* (SOH-kah-loh).

The public square, or *zócalo*, is the center of most villages, towns, and cities in Mexico. People go there to visit, hear speeches, celebrate special occasions, or go to church.

You Can Make Mexican Crepe-Paper Flowers

What You Need • Tissue paper in bright colors • Scissors • Pipe cleaners (green or different colors)

What to Do

1. Cut six sheets of tissue paper (same or different colors) into 12-inch (30-centimeter) squares.

2. Stack the squares neatly.

3. Taking the whole stack at once, make a 1-inch (2½-centimeter) fold along one edge. Run your thumb over the fold to crease it.

4. Flip the stack over and make another 1-inch (2½-centimeter) fold the other way, as if you are making a fan.

5. Continue to flip the stack over and make 1-inch (2½-centimeter) folds until the fan is complete.

6. Twist a pipe cleaner around the center of the fan. For a short stem, make the twist in the middle of the pipe cleaner. For a longer stem, make the twist at one end.

7. Trim the corners of the fan, making them rounded.

8. Bring the two ends of the fan together. Hold the fan tightly at the base, where it attaches to the pipe cleaner. Carefully begin to peel back the layers of tissue paper, from the outside in, until you have a fluffy flower.

9. Use these flowers to decorate your party table. Set one at each place, or arrange a few in a vase.

Say It in Spanish

good morning	*buenos días*	(BWAY-nohss DEE-ahss)
good-bye	*adiós*	(ah-dee-OHSS)
please	*por favor*	(POR fah-VOR)
thank you	*gracias*	(GRAH-see-ahss)
boy	*el niño*	(el NEE-nyoh)
girl	*la niña*	(lah NEE-nyah)

Fast Facts

Official name:	The United Mexican States
Capital:	Mexico City
Official language:	Spanish
Population:	101,879,171
Area:	761,602 square miles (1,972,550 square kilometers)
Highest point:	Volcano Pico de Orizaba, 18,700 feet (5,700 meters)
Lowest point:	Laguna Salada, 33 feet (10 meters) below sea level
Type of government:	republic
Head of government:	president
Major industries:	food products, iron and steel, textiles, tourism
Natural resources:	timber, copper, gold, petroleum
Major agricultural products:	fruits, vegetables, cacao, coffee
Chief exports:	oil and oil products, silver, cotton, coffee
National bird:	crested caracara
National flower:	dahlia

Fun Facts

• Mexico has over 1,000 volcanoes. Some are active and could erupt at any time.

• Sapodilla trees in southern Mexico provide *chicle* (CHEE-klay), a gooey material used to make chewing gum.

• One of the world's smallest dogs, the chihuahua, originally came from Mexico. Mexico's largest state and that state's capital city are named Chihuahua.

• Mexicans love soccer, which they call *futbol* (FOOT-bohl).

Glossary

adobe (uh-DOH-bee)—bricks made of mud and straw, dried and hardened by the heat of the sun

luminaria (loo-mih-NAIR-ee-ah)—a traditional Mexican Christmas lantern

mariachi (mair-ee-AH-chee)—a lively style of dance music, or the name for bands that play this type of music

mural (MYU-ruhl)—a painting on a wall

peninsula (puh-NIN-suh-luh)—a piece of land with water on three sides

piñata (pee-NYAH-tah)—a colorful container, usually made of paper, that is filled with treats for parties

serape (say-RAH-pay)—a colorful woolen shawl or blanket

tortilla (tor-TEE-yah)—round, thin, flat wheat or corn bread

traditional (truh-DISH-uh-nul)—handed down from one generation to another within a family or culture

To Learn More

At the Library

Auch, Alison. *Welcome to Mexico.* Minneapolis: Compass Point Books, 2002.

Beatty, Theresa M. *Food and Recipes of Mexico.* New York: Power Kids Press, 1999.

Ehlert, Lois. *Cuckoo: A Mexican Folktale = Cucú: Un Cuento Folklórico Mexicano.* San Diego: Harcourt Brace, 1997.

Kimmel, Eric A. *The Two Mountains: An Aztec Legend.* New York: Holiday House, 2000.

Madrigal, Antonio Hernandez. *Erandi's Braids.* New York: Putnam's, 1999.

Fact Hound

Fact Hound offers a safe, fun way to find Web sites related to this book. All of the sites on Fact Hound have been researched by our staff.
http://www.facthound.com

1. Visit the Fact Hound home page.
2. Enter a search word related to this book, or type in this special code: 1404800239.
3. Click the FETCH IT button.

Your trusty Fact Hound will fetch the best sites for you!

Index

animals, 5, 9, 14, 20

art, 4

Aztecs. *See* people

capital. *See* Mexico City

Caribbean Sea, 3, 27

celebrations. *See* holidays

Chichen Itza, 27

clothing, 22

coat of arms, 9

exports, 30

flag, 9

food, 8, 23, 30

government, 13, 30

Guadalupe, Virgin of, 25

holidays

    Christmas, 15

    Cinco de Mayo, 6

    Day of the Dead, 7

    Independence Day, 6

houses, 11

Juárez, Benito, 13

language, 3, 24, 29, 30

maps, 3

Mayas, *See* people

Mexico City, 9, 30

Mexico, Gulf of, 3, 21, 27

money *(peso)*, 16

Montezuma II, 26

music, 10

native peoples. *See* people

natural features

    desert, 14, 17

    mountains, 5, 14

    oceans/sea, 3, 14, 27

    rain forest, 14, 20

    river, 21

    volcanoes, 30

North America, 3

people

    Aztecs, 4, 9, 20, 26

    Mayas, 4, 27

    Spanish (Spaniards), 4, 12, 21

    Zapotecs, 4, 13

piñata, 19

plants, 5, 17, 26

population, 3, 30

religion, 12, 25, 28

Río Grande, 21

Spain, 4, 6

Spanish (Spaniards). *See* people

tourism, 26, 27

Virgin of Guadalupe. *See* Guadalupe, Virgin of

Xochimilco, Lake, 26

Yucatan Peninsula, 27

Zapotecs. *See* people